THOMAS JEFFERSON
A BRIEF BIOGRAPHY

Thomas Jefferson
A BRIEF BIOGRAPHY

Dumas Malone

Preface by Merrill D. Peterson

THOMAS JEFFERSON FOUNDATION

Monticello Monograph Series

The Thomas Jefferson Foundation, Inc.

This book was made possible by support from the
Martin S. and Luella Davis Publications Endowment.

Reprinted with permission by
the Thomas Jefferson Foundation.

Dumas Malone's initial essay on Jefferson was published in 1933 in
Volume X of the *Dictionary of American Biography*. Malone later revised this
essay for publication in *Thomas Jefferson: a Reference Biography* (1986), edited
by Merrill D. Peterson. This book is a reprint of the 1986 revision.

On the cover:
Thomas Jefferson by Charles Willson Peale (courtesy Independence National Historical
Park) and the west elevation of Monticello drawn by Robert Mills about 1803 (courtesy
Massachusetts Historical Society, N154/K155. MHS Image #1158).

Designed by Gibson Design Associates.
Printed by GraphTec, Annapolis Junction, Maryland.

Distributed by the University of North Carolina Press
Chapel Hill, North Carolina 27515-2288
1-800-848-6224

H G F E
ISBN 1-882886-00-3

PREFACE

D UMAS MALONE first crossed Jefferson's path when he was a graduate student at Yale, working on a doctoral dissertation suggested by his mentor, Allen Johnson. Malone, a native Mississippian, had come to Yale as a divinity student but after serving in the Marine Corps in World War I he returned to New Haven and began the study of American history. Johnson guided Malone as he wrote a life of Thomas Cooper, an English political exile who came to America and became a close friend of Jefferson's. As he worked on the Cooper biography, Malone was introduced to the Jefferson Papers at the Library of Congress and he saw that Cooper was a prickly character who lived in a state of commotion; certainly, he was hardly a congenial subject for Malone, whose temperament was mild and who had little taste for controversy. But Jefferson and Cooper were philosophical friends—a relationship of contrasting temperaments not unlike that between Malone and Cooper as author and subject. Indeed, Jefferson had offered Cooper a professorship at the emerging University of Virginia, then had to withdraw the offer in the face of public outcry against Cooper as a Unitarian and agitator.

Malone finished his dissertation and in 1922 he was offered a teaching position at Virginia, and unlike Cooper he was welcomed to Charlottesville. "I fell in love with Jefferson's 'academical village,' at first sight," Malone would recall in his memoirs. In time Malone decided to undertake a biography of Jefferson, and in preparation for his task he edited the Jefferson–Du Pont de Nemours correspondence, which appeared in 1930. Meanwhile, his Yale mentor had beckoned to Malone to join him on the staff of the scholarly *Dictionary of American Biography*, a multi-volumed work that would bring together biographies of all prominent Americans over three centuries. But tragedy befell Johnson, he was killed in a traffic accident in Washington; and the role of editor-in-chief was conferred on Malone. He had already started work on his "coveted assignment," a 15,000-word biography of Jefferson, but he had to postpone its completion as he mustered over two thousand contributors into a working team. Eventually, the project was finished in 1936 only six months behind schedule, with 13,633 articles. Many critics thought Malone's article on Jefferson was full of sound information and insight, and among the best of all the articles that crossed Malone's desk.

Malone went on to several career mileposts, at Harvard University and Columbia University, but he kept alive the Jeffersonian spark in his bosom and projected a full biography of the Virginian he had come to admire. A contract signed in 1938 would bind Malone to his happy task, and beginning in 1948 the volumes began to appear, with the general title: *Jefferson and His Time*. The first volume, *Jefferson the Virginian*, won critical acclaim and in 1951 *Jefferson and the Rights of Man* established Malone as the preeminent Jefferson scholar. He resumed his affiliation at the University of Virginia and in 1962 he was named biographer-in-residence, a title he cherished until his death late in 1986, just two weeks before his ninety-fifth birthday.

Malone had, in the intervening decades, won the Pulitzer prize for his fifth volume in 1974, and he capped the six-volume work with the magisterial *The Sage of Monticello*, published on July 4, 1981.

While I was preparing a manuscript for the book *Thomas Jefferson: A Reference Biography* I asked Malone if he would look at his sketch from the *Dictionary of American Biography* and make any revisions needed, then allow me to publish it in my work. Generosity was Malone's hallmark, and he readily consented to revise his groundbreaking biographical essay. The result is printed in this volume, and represents the encapsuled wisdom of Malone as he viewed and wrote about one of America's greatest citizens. In the fifty years since Malone had written his essay, he came to realize that he had "conceded more to Jefferson's opponents and critics than I afterwards saw any need to do." With great relish Malone amended his earlier work and he hewed to his own standard by viewing Jefferson not "as a static personality like a portrait on the wall, but as a living, growing, changing man—always the same person but never quite the same."

Late in life Malone was troubled by admirers who suggested that he had become Mr. Jefferson reincarnate. He was too good a scholar, and too strong a person in his own right, to confuse himself with his subject. Yet precisely because his intellect and personality permeated his understanding of Jefferson, Malone had made himself virtually inseparable from our own image of the man. In this brief biography, readers will see the Jefferson who was revisited by Malone after half a century of intense study of the third president's life. Here, in shortened form, is a tale told with great respect but not without an effort to avoid hero worship. In this short work, the reader will become acquainted with the mind and temperament of Thomas Jefferson as written by the greatest Jefferson scholar in our history. How fitting that as we celebrate the 250th anniversary of Jefferson's birth, Malone's little jewel of a biography becomes a part of that celebration.

— MERRILL D. PETERSON
Charlottesville, Virginia
December, 1992

Jefferson while Secretary of State, painted by Charles Willson Peale in December 1791. (Independence National Historical Park.)

THOMAS JEFFERSON, statesman, diplomat, author, scientist, architect, apostle of freedom and enlightenment, was born on 13 April 1743, at Shadwell, in what is now Albemarle County, Virginia, then on the fringe of western settlement. Whether or not the first Jefferson in the colony came from Wales, as the family tradition held, a Thomas Jefferson was living in Henrico County in 1679 and married Mary Branch. Their son Thomas, who married Mary Field, lived at Osbornes in the present Chesterfield County, where on the last day of February 1707/1708 Peter Jefferson was born. His father was a "gentleman Justice," but Peter enjoyed few educational opportunities and had largely to shift for himself. Becoming a surveyor, he moved to Goochland County, where by 1734 he was a magistrate. The next year he patented a thousand acres on the south side of the Rivanna River and shortly thereafter, "for a bowl of punch," purchased from William Randolph of the plantation of Tuckahoe four hundred acres more. This contained the site north of the river upon which he erected a plain frame house in about 1741. Thither he brought his wife, and there Thomas, his third child, was born.

Jane Randolph, who became Peter Jefferson's wife at nineteen, first cousin of William of Tuckahoe and the eldest surviving child of Isham Randolph of Dungeness and his wife, Jane Rogers, connected her husband with one of the most distinguished families in the province and assured the social standing of his children. Peter Jefferson's career closely followed that of Joshua Fry, under whom he served as deputy surveyor in Albemarle, with whom he completed the boundary line between Virginia and North Carolina and made the first accurate map of Virginia, and whom he succeeded as burgess and county lieutenant. Thomas Jefferson had great respect for his father's map and from him may have acquired his zest for exploring and drawing and his liking for untrodden paths. From him he inherited a vigorous, if less powerful, body and perhaps his fondness for mathematical subjects. Of the ten children of Peter Jefferson, eight survived him. He left Thomas, the elder of his two sons, about five thousand acres of land and an established position in the community.

Seven of the first nine years of Jefferson's life were spent at Tuckahoe, on the James a few miles above the present Richmond, whither his father moved in fulfillment of a promise to William Randolph to act as guardian of the latter's son. Here Thomas began his education at the "English school." The red hills of Albemarle became his permanent home, however, at the age of nine and held evermore an unrivaled place in his affections. Soon thereafter he began the study of Latin and Greek under the Reverend William Douglas, who also introduced him to French. Of Douglas' abilities he later expressed a low opinion. After the death of his father, he studied with the Reverend James Maury, whom he later described as "a correct classical scholar." Jefferson gained an early mastery of the classical tongues and ever found the literature of Greece and Rome a "rich source of delight." In March 1760 he entered the College of William and Mary, from which he was graduated two years later. At Williamsburg, the provincial capital, he was able to view history in the making and government in practice. His chief intellectual stimulus while a student came from his association with William Small, who held the chair of mathematics and ad interim that of natural philosophy. Small aroused in him the interest in scientific questions that was destined to remain active all his life. Small introduced him to the "familiar table" of Governor Francis Fauquier and to George Wythe, most noted teacher of law of his generation in Virginia, under whose guidance he prepared himself for practice.

During these years Jefferson was a recognized member of the close-knit social group that the children of the ruling gentry of Virginia constituted. He visited homes, made wagers with girls, gossiped about love affairs, served at weddings. Tall, loose-jointed, sandy-haired, and freckled, he was not prepossessing in appearance, but he was a skilled horseman, played on the violin, and seems to have been a gay companion. The strain of seriousness in his nature was soon apparent, however. It may have been accentuated by the unhappy outcome of his love affair with Rebecca Burwell, an "affair" largely carried out in his imagination. Before he became a prominent actor on the stage of public life, he had formulated for himself a stern code of personal conduct and had disciplined himself to habits of study as few of his contemporaries ever found strength to do. Sometime after 1764, perhaps, he began to apply historical tests to the Bible, lost faith in conventional religion, though without questioning conventional morality, and for inspiration turned to the great classical writers. Finding these insufficient in later years, he found ethical guidance in the teachings of Jesus. That he prepared himself with unusual care for his profession, by the study of legal history as well as of procedure, is shown by the notebook in which he abridged his legal reading. He was admitted to the bar in 1767 and despite his dislike of court practice, was distinctly successful in the law until, on the eve of the Revolution, he abandoned it as a profession.

On 1 January 1772, Jefferson was married to Martha (Wayles) Skelton, then in her twenty-fourth year, the daughter of John Wayles of Charles City County and his wife, Martha Eppes. She was the widow of Bathurst Skelton and had borne him a son, who died shortly before her marriage to Jefferson. In the ten years of their married life she bore Jefferson six children, only three of whom survived her and only two of whom, Martha and Mary (or Maria), attained maturity. She is reputed to have been beautiful, and certainly her second husband lavished upon her notable devotion. The young couple began their married life in the only part of Monticello then finished, the southeastern pavilion. Jefferson had moved to his adored mountaintop after the house at Shadwell burned, together with his cherished library, in 1770, and had begun the building operations which were to extend over a generation. From the estate of his father-in-law he acquired in behalf of his wife, soon after his marriage, holdings roughly equivalent to his own. With them, however, went a huge debt from the effects of which he never entirely escaped. Throughout most of his mature life he was the owner of approximately ten thousand acres of land and between one hundred and two hundred slaves. Nothing if not methodical, he made periodical records of everything connected with his plantations—his slaves, his horses and cattle, the trees planted, the temperature at Monticello, the dates on which birds and flowers first appeared.

In 1770, Jefferson was appointed county lieutenant of Albemarle. In May 1769 he had become a member of the House of Burgesses, and he continued to be one until the House ceased to function in 1775, though he did not attend in 1772. He says he had been intimate for almost a decade with Patrick Henry, whose eloquence had enthralled him in his student days. Never an effective public speaker, Jefferson himself did greatest service in legislative bodies on committees, where his marked talents as a literary draftsman were employed. Identified from the outset with the aggressive anti-British group, he was one of those who drew up the resolves creating the Virginia Committee of Correspondence and was appointed a member of the committee of eleven, though not of the select committee of three. In 1774 he was one of the champions of the resolution for a fast day, on the day the Boston Port Act was to go into effect. This resolution led to the dissolution of the House. In 1775 he was on the committee appointed to draw up an address to the earl of Dunmore, the royal governor, rejecting Lord North's conciliatory offer, and he says that he drafted the address adopted. Prevented by illness from attending the Virginia convention of 1774, he sent a paper that was later published as *A Summary View of the Rights of British America*. This proved to be his greatest literary contribution to the American Revolution next to the Declaration of Independence, and it reveals, as perhaps no other document does, his point of view in that struggle. Though approved by many, it was not adopted because it was regarded as too advanced. Emphasizing the "natural" right of emigration exercised by the first English settlers in America as by the Saxon settlers in England, he denied all parliamentary authority over the colonies. He claimed that the only political tie with Great Britain was supplied by the king, to whom the colonists had voluntarily submitted. He believed that the assistance rendered by the mother country to the colonists had been solely for commercial benefit and was repayable only in trade privileges. This powerful pamphlet, distinctly legalistic in tone, reveals no adequate conception of the value of early English protection or of the contemporary British imperial problem. Throughout his career as a Revolutionary patriot he emphasized "rights as derived from the laws of nature," not a king; and here, as elsewhere, he strove for the "revindication of Saxon liberties."

Elected by the Virginia convention to serve in Congress in case Peyton Randolph should be required at home, Jefferson sat in that body during the summer and autumn of 1775. Though he drafted several papers, these were too strongly anti-British in tone to be acceptable while there was hope of conciliation. He was not present in Congress from 28 December 1775 to 14 May 1776. Probably called home by the illness of his mother, who died 31 March, and by the needs of his family, he also had duties to perform as county lieutenant and commander of the militia of Albemarle, to which office he had been appointed by the Virginia Committee of Safety on 26 September. Following the famous resolutions introduced into Congress on 7 June 1776 by Richard Henry Lee, Jefferson was elected four days later, with John Adams, Benjamin Franklin, Roger Sherman, and Robert R. Livingston, to a committee to draw up a declaration of independence. The reasons for the prominence in this connection of one so young as Jefferson

A miniature likeness of Jefferson's eldest daughter, Martha Jefferson Randolph, was painted on ivory by the French artist Joseph Boze in 1789. (Diplomatic Reception Rooms, United States Department of State.)

have been much disputed. It was inevitable that a Virginian should be on the committee, and Richard Henry Lee had gone home. Now only thirty-three years old, Jefferson had been a "silent member" on the floor of Congress, though outspoken and decisive in committees. The "reputation of a masterly pen" stood him in good stead and opened to him the door of dangerous but glorious opportunity.

More changes in his draft of the Declaration were made at the instance of Franklin and Adams than he remembered, and some were made by Congress itself; but the most famous American political document as a composition belongs indisputably to Jefferson. The philosophical portion strikingly resembles the first three sections of George Mason's Declaration of Rights, itself a notable summary of current revolutionary philosophy. Jefferson probably availed himself of this, but he improved upon it. The doctrines are essentially those of John Locke, in which the more radical of the patriots were steeped. Jefferson himself did not believe in absolute human equality, and though he had no fears of revolution, he preferred that the "social compact" be renewed by periodical, peaceful revisions. He steadfastly believed that government should be based on popular consent and secure the "inalienable" rights of man, among which he included the pursuit of

Jefferson dominates Asher B. Durand's engraving (1823) of John Trumbull's painting The Declaration of Independence. *(Thomas Jefferson Foundation.)*

happiness rather than property, that government should be a means to human well-being and not an end in itself. He gave here a matchless expression of his faith. The charges against the king, who is singled out because all claims of parliamentary authority are implicitly denied, are in general an improved version of those that had already been drawn up by Jefferson and adopted as the preamble of the Virginia constitution of 1776. Relentless in their reiteration, they constitute a statement of the specific grievances of the revolting party, powerfully and persuasively presented at the bar of public opinion. The Declaration is notable for both its clarity and its subtlety of expression, and it abounds in the felicities that are characteristic of Jefferson's unlabored prose. It is eloquent in its sustained elevation of style and remains his noblest literary monument.

Desiring to be nearer his family and believing that he could be more useful in furthering the reformation of Virginia than in Congress, Jefferson left the latter body in September 1776 and, entering the Virginia House of Delegates on 7 October, served there until his election to the governorship in June 1779. While a member of Congress, he had submitted to the Virginia convention of 1776 a constitution and preamble, only the latter of which had been adopted. With the new constitution and government, which were marked by little change in law and social organization, he was soon profoundly dissatisfied. To him the Revolution meant more than a redress of grievances. Against the continuance of an established church, divorced from England, which the conservatives favored, he desired the entire separation of church and state. He was determined to rid his "country," as he called Virginia, of the artificial aristocracy of wealth and birth and to facilitate through education the development of a natural aristocracy of talent and virtue and of an enlightened electorate. He believed that the legal code should be adapted to republican government "with a single eye to reason, & the good of those for whose government it was formed." Because of his skill as a legislator, the definiteness of his carefully formulated program, and the almost religious zeal with which he pressed it, he immediately assumed the leadership of the progressive group. He deserves the chief credit not only for an unparalleled program but also for legislative achievements that have rarely been equaled in American history.

He struck the first blow at the aristocratic system by procuring the abolition of landholding in fee tail. On 12 October 1776 he moved the revision of the laws. Elected to the board of revisers with four others, of whom only George Wythe and Edmund Pendleton served to the end, he labored two years with scholarly thoroughness on his share of the revision, including the law of descent and the criminal law. The report of the board (18 June 1779) consisted of 126 bills, most of which were ultimately enacted in substance. Primogeniture was abolished in 1785. His Bill for Establishing Religious Freedom, presented in 1779 by John Harvie of Albemarle and passed, with slight but significant modifications in the preamble in 1786 when Jefferson was in France, was regarded by him as one of his greatest contributions to humanity. In its assertion that the mind is not subject to coercion, that civil rights have no dependence on religious opinions, and that the opinions of men are not the concern of civil government, it is indeed one of the great American charters of freedom.

Jefferson's educational bills, which represented the constructive part of his program, were unsuccessful. Of his extraordinary Bill for the More General Diffusion of Knowledge, which summarizes his educational philosophy, only the part dealing with elementary schools was acted on (in 1796), and a provision was inserted that defeated its purpose. His attempts to amend the constitution of his old college and to establish a public library entirely failed. During his governorship, however, he effected the abolishment of the professorships of Hebrew, theology, and ancient languages and the establishment of professorships of anatomy and medicine, law, and modern languages, the two latter being the first of their kind of America. Though he did not originate the idea of removing the capital to Richmond, he framed a bill for that purpose and the measure that was passed in 1779 included his preamble and provisions for handsome public buildings such as he had favored.

On 1 June 1779, Jefferson was elected governor of Virginia by the General Assembly. His term was one year, and he was reelected for another. The qualities of mind that made him so conspicuous a planner and prophet were of slight avail to him as a wartime administrator. He had little power. Under the state constitution of 1776, he could not veto legislation, and his actions were subject to the approval of the Council of State, a body of eight men who were elected by the Assembly. He presided over this group but could vote only in case of a tie. He was not disposed to overstep his constitutional bounds, but his experience in this office caused him to oppose legislative dominance ever afterward.

This agricultural society suffered during the war from the loss of the British market for tobacco, and the wheat crop was almost wholly destroyed by drought in Jefferson's first year as governor. For money, the legislators turned to the printing press. By the time Jefferson left office, the currency was said to have had little more value than oak leaves. Under these difficult circumstances, he was unceasing in his efforts to meet the requisitions of the Continental Congress, to raise troops, and to procure arms and supplies.

In the autumn of 1780, weary and frustrated, he talked privately of resigning and certainly had no desire to serve a third year. Thus far, the state had been spared invasion; and its military resources had been drained to strengthen armies elsewhere. In the first days of 1781, Benedict Arnold made a surprise raid into the interior from the coast. He did little damage in Richmond, which had recently become the capital, but he set fire to the foundry six miles upstream, where arms were stored. After the governor was reliably informed that Arnold was coming, he was tireless in his effort to protect the property of the state, but he did not call the militia in time to oppose the invader, and he was afterward charged with slowness and indecision. The advance of Cornwallis from the south in the spring with an overpowering force was far more serious. This occasioned the precipitate flight of the entire state government and its virtual dissolution.

The legislators who gathered in Richmond on 10 May for their annual spring session adjourned to meet later in Charlottesville, seventy miles to the west; there on 28 May they attained a quorum. The election of a governor was scheduled for Saturday, 2 June, when Jefferson's second year would end, but unfortunately was postponed until Monday. That morning Lt. Col. Banastre Tarleton and a large body of British horsemen entered Charlottesville. Cornwallis had sent him to upset the Assembly. Jefferson had as guests at Monticello the Speakers of the two houses and other legislators. There could be no meeting of the Council of State, because there were not enough councillors, but he wrote some last official letters.

Before dawn on Monday, a gigantic horseman rode up the mountainside. Capt. Jack Jouett had made a heroic ride through the night to warn Jefferson and the Assembly. The aroused delegates met in Charlottesville, voted to adjourn to Staunton across the mountain, and fled precipitately in that direction. They did not wait to elect a governor. Jefferson sent his family to Blenheim, an estate in the southern part of the county. He himself remained at Monticello until he could actually see Redcoats through his telescope. Then he rode through the woods to Blenheim. Later he took his family to Poplar Forest, his place in Bedford County.

What was left of the General Assembly, meeting at Staunton, finally got around to the election of a governor. By choosing Gen. Thomas Nelson, the ranking officer of the militia, they joined the civil and military authorities. On the same day (12 June 1781) the House of Delegates adopted a resolution calling for an investigation of the conduct of the recent executive at the next session. No specific charges were made at this or any other time. Judging from what Jefferson learned from the author of the resolution, George Nicholas, during the summer, that delegate was not thinking of Tarleton's raid, which actually appears to have frightened the legislators more than it did Jefferson, but of the raid of Benedict Arnold. It was his official conduct in the earlier raid, not the later, that the former governor defended at the legislative session in the fall. By this time the invasion of the state by Cornwallis had ended with his surrender, and there was no need to blame anybody for the sufferings of the past.

On 12 December the committee appointed by the House of Delegates to inquire into the conduct of the recent executive reported that no information had been offered them except rumors, which they regarded as groundless. A week later, resolutions of thanks to Jefferson were adopted by both houses. Formally vindicated, Jefferson soon recovered his prestige in Virginia. His election as delegate to the Continental Congress at this session of the legislature—an election he declined—showed that he retained public confidence. The chief significance of the closing events of his ill-fated governorship lay in the relatively distant future, when he was involved in national contests. Then these events were distorted out of all reason in the effort of political enemies to show that he was unfit to be president of the United States. By then his skin appears to have become a little tougher than it was in 1781. Despite the handsome amends his fellow Virginians then made for unjust criticism, he was convinced that public service and private misery were inseparable. Accordingly he had retired to his neglected farms, his cherished books, and his beloved family, convinced that nothing could again separate him from them.

Jefferson took advantage of the leisure forced upon him by a fall from his horse to organize the careful memoranda about Virginia that he had made over a long period. Arranging these in the order of the queries submitted in 1781 by François de Barbé-Marbois, secretary of the French legation, he somewhat corrected and enlarged them during the winter of 1782-1783 and had them printed in France in 1785. The *Notes on the State of Virginia* went through many editions and laid the foundations of Jefferson's high contemporary reputation as a universal scholar and of his enduring fame as a pioneer American scientist. Unpretentious in form and statistical in character, this unusually informative and generally interesting book may still be consulted with profit about the geography and productions, and the social and political life, of eighteenth-century Virginia. With ardent patriotism as well as zeal for truth, Jefferson combated the theories of Buffon and Raynal in regard to the inferiority of animal and intellectual life in America, and he manifested great optimism in regard to the future of the country, but he included "strictures" on slavery and the government of Virginia. In 1783 he drafted another proposed constitution for his state, which was published in 1786 and ultimately bound with the *Notes* as an appendix.

But for the death of his wife on 6 September 1782, he might have remained in philosophic retirement. He lavished upon his motherless daughters extraordinary tenderness and solicitude, but he was now glad to abandon Monticello and seek relief from personal woe in public activity. Appointed peace commissioner to Europe on 12 November 1782, he was prepared to sail when, his mission having become unnecessary, his appointment was withdrawn. In June 1783 he was elected a delegate to Congress, and during six months' service in that body the following winter he was a member of almost every important committee and drafted an extraordinary number of state papers. Some of these were of the first importance, especially his notes on the coinage, in which he advocated the adoption of the dollar, to be divided into tenths and hundredths, and his successive reports on the government of the western territory. The reports of 22 March 1784 contained most of the features of the epoch-making Ordinance of 1787. If it had been adopted as Jefferson presented it, slavery would have been forbidden in all the western territory after 1800, and the secession of any part of that region would have been rendered indisputably illegal. Jefferson had earlier drafted a deed of cession of the north-western territory that was claimed by Virginia, and he drew up a land ordinance that failed of adoption. Certainly he was a major architect of American expansion. He also drafted a report on the definitive treaty of peace that was eventually adopted. On 20 December 1783 he drew up a report that was agreed to as the basis of procedure in the negotiation of treaties of commerce and was himself appointed, on 7 May 1784, to assist Franklin and Adams in this work in Europe.

Joining them in Paris on 6 August, with his daughter Martha, he was appointed in 1785 Franklin's successor as minister to France and remained in that country until October 1789. Rightly regarded in France as a savant, he carried on the tradition of Franklin, but until the end of his own stay he was overshadowed by Franklin's immense reputation. Jefferson's attitude toward his predecessor, whom he regarded as one of the two greatest Americans (the other being George Washington), was one of becoming modesty without a tinge of jealousy. During his ministry he was somewhat overshadowed by Lafayette, who was regarded as the French symbol of American ideals and the protector of American interests. Jefferson took full advantage of Lafayette's invaluable cooperation and associated with him on terms of intimacy and affection, content to be relatively inconspicuous if he might be useful.

Though he later characterized his official activities in France as unimportant, he proved a diligent and skillful diplomat. He and his colleagues succeeded in negotiating, in 1785, a treaty of commerce with Prussia. Early in 1786 he joined Adams in London, but their efforts to negotiate a commercial treaty with Great Britain were futile. He took careful note of English domestic gardening and mechanical appliances, but of English architecture and manners had few kind words to say. He supported Thomas Barclay in the negotiation of a treaty with Morocco in 1787 but was convinced that the Barbary pirates could be restrained only by force and worked out a scheme for concerted action on the part of a league of nations. This was accepted by Congress but aroused no enthusiasm in Europe. He negotiated with France a consular convention, signed 14 November 1788, which was the first of the sort agreed to by the United States. Though he could not hope to make much of a breach in the wall of commercial exclusiveness, he gained some relaxation of French duties on American products and, by his arguments against the tobacco monopoly of the Farmers-General, made a definite impression on Vergennes and his successor, Montmorin. Jefferson left Europe with the belief that the French had granted all the commercial concessions possible at the time, that they had few interests in America, and that they had great sentimental attachment to the young republic. He was convinced that the United States should be friendly to France, both because of gratitude and because of France's value as a counterpoise against the British, whom he regarded as hostile in sentiment and entirely selfish in policy. He gained the impression, however, that Great Britain and Spain would pay much for American neutrality if they should become involved in European controversy. The hope that the United States would ultimately gain great advantages from the troubles of Europe profoundly affected his subsequent foreign policy, predisposing him to ways of peace.

At a time when there was a flood of sentimental French writings about America, Jefferson endeavored to present the American cause adequately and accurately. These motives in part caused him to distribute his own *Notes on the State of Virginia* and the Virginia Statute for Religious Freedom. Not only did he respond generously to inquiries about America, but he shared freely with his own countrymen the knowledge he himself gained of another world. To interested friends at home, he wrote about inventions in dozens of letters; and for Madison, Monroe, and others he continually purchased books. In 1787, on an extensive journey through the French provinces, he made a careful study of vineyards, and he went into northern Italy to see the machines used there for cleaning rice. He sent samples of upland rice seed to South Carolina and Georgia and forwarded information about the olive tree. At Nîmes he gazed for hours on the Maison

Carrée, "like a lover at his mistress." For the new state capitol of Virginia, he sent a plan modeled on this temple and thus initiated the classical revival in American architecture. On a tour in 1788, he made numerous observations in Germany. This keen-eyed, reflective traveler purposed that his mission should prove educational to his fellow citizens as well as to himself and never lost sight of his obligation to be useful.

He was greatly impressed with the manners of the French though opposed to any aping of them by Americans, and he was attracted by French cuisine and wines. He found the French a temperate people but believed the life of the upper classes to be lacking in domestic happiness and rather futile on the whole. He was appalled by the poverty he observed among the lower classes. He thought little of the science of the French but was enthusiastic about their arts—architecture, painting, and music. Perhaps he valued music the more because a fractured wrist had ended his days as a violinist. Distressed by the oppression and inequality he observed in the Old World, he came to think less than ever of kings, nobles, and priests. His experience in France did not give him a new political and social philosophy. It confirmed the basic views he already had and stimulated his democratic faith. He shared the belief of the *philosophes* in the indefinite improvability of mankind and made a virtual religion of enlightenment. He also had a first-hand knowledge of the operations of representative government, which the French reformers lacked. He correctly perceived that this society was far from ready for self-government of the American variety, and he never ceased to fear that the reformers would attempt too much and promote a reaction.

The course of the French Revolution until his departure Jefferson followed closely and reported in detail. Though he strove to maintain strict official propriety, this skilled political architect privately suggested to Lafayette's aunt, Madame de Tessé, a desirable course of procedure for the Assembly of Notables, and to Lafayette himself he submitted a proposed charter for France. A meeting of the leaders of the Patriot party, arranged by Lafayette, was held at Jefferson's house in the effort to arrive at a compromise on the questions of the royal veto and the constitution of the Assembly. Jefferson commented on successive drafts of a declaration of rights by Lafayette and through him may have had some influence on the famous Declaration of the Rights of Man and the Citizens. He rejoiced in the adoption of this great charter of individual freedom and had high hopes that the revolt against tyranny in France would be followed by the establishment of a firm government. In revolutionary France, however, he was distinctly a moderate. He now believed that the reformers should be content with a limited monarchy, and he never ceased to regard the execution of Louis XVI (1793) as a crucial mistake. The French Revolution became a burning issue in American politics, and his discriminating attitude was not understood by many at that time and thereafter. Toward the end of his life, he said that nothing was immutable but the "inherent and inalienable rights of man." So long as the French Revolution served to support and advance these rights, he strongly approved of it. But he deplored the tyranny of Robespierre as well as that of Napoleon.

This counselor of moderation was strongly opposed to the counterrevolution, and he favored the adjustment of laws and institutions to the inevitable changes in human affairs. In a letter he wrote Madison shortly before his departure from France (6 September 1789), he denied the right of one generation to bind another. "The earth belongs always to the living generation," he said. In particular, he denied the right of a government, such as that of France, to transmit to posterity a heavy burden of debt. His objection to certain features of Alexander Hamilton's financial policy a few years later and his persistent effort to reduce the national debt after he became president were both grounded on what he regarded as a moral principle. He also asserted that any and every generation has the right to be governed by laws of its own making. He argued that constitutions should be revised every nineteen years. Cogent arguments against this impracticable procedure were duly presented to him by Madison, but he appears to have forgotten these, for he revived the idea when seeking to modernize the Virginia constitution in his old age.

Having been granted a leave of absence to settle his private affairs and to take home his two daughters, the younger of whom, Mary, had joined him in Paris in 1787, Jefferson sailed in October 1789 and arrived at Monticello two days before Christmas, to be welcomed tumultuously by his slaves. Soon after he landed, he received from President George Washington the offer of appointment as secretary of state, a post that was being temporarily filled by John Jay. Jefferson's dislike for publicity and shrinking from censure made him reluctant to enter the storm of politics, from which in France he had been relatively aloof, but on patriotic grounds he eventually accepted the eminently appropriate appointment. After giving his daughter Martha in marriage to her cousin

Thomas Mann Randolph, Jr., he proceeded to New York, where, in March 1790, he became the first secretary of state under the Constitution.

Although he had kept in touch with American developments through extensive correspondence, Jefferson was not fully aware of the conservative reaction that had taken place in his own country while he was in the midst of political ferment in France. He had seen nothing threatening in the commotions that had marked the last years of the Confederation and, in any event, thought dangerous liberty distinctly preferable to quiet slavery. Despite the imperfections of the government, he had described it as "without comparison the best existing or that ever did exist." Nonetheless, he had viewed with favor the movement for strengthening the federal government and had given the new Constitution his general approval, objecting chiefly to the absence of a bill of rights, which was later supplied, and the perpetual reeligibility of the president. He had denied that he was of the party of Federalists but had stated that he was much farther from the Anti-Federalists. Before his retirement from office, he came to be regarded as the leader of the group opposed to the policies of Alexander Hamilton. To distinguish themselves from their opponents, whom they termed "monarchists," Jefferson and his sympathizers called themselves "republicans." Until the end of his life, he believed that his early fears of an American monarchy were warranted. Undoubtedly he was distressed by the change in the political atmosphere in which he found himself. In the aristocratic Federalist court, at first in New York and soon in Philadelphia, this accomplished gentleman was ill at ease.

With Hamilton, who was nearly a dozen years his junior and had already assumed the first place in the councils of the government, he strove at the outset to cooperate. His subsequent statement that he was duped by his colleague in connection with the bill for federal assumption of state debts incurred by the Revolution is unconvincing. His contemporary letters clearly show that he believed at the time that some compromise was essential for peace and the preservation of the Union. When at length better provision for Virginia was made in the bill and the location of the federal city on the banks of the Potomac was agreed to, he gave his approval to the measure. While Jefferson may already have perceived that Hamilton was catering to a new moneyed group and was relatively indifferent to the agricultural interests, he had shown no particular disapproval of his colleague's financial policies as yet. He was always fearful of centralized government, but he was not yet fully aware that there was danger of the concentration of power in Hamilton's own person.

The first serious difference of opinion between the two men was over a question of foreign policy. Fully convinced that the British would not yield their posts in the old Northwest or grant commercial privileges unless forced to do so, Jefferson favored the employment of commercial discrimination as a weapon against them. This policy, advocated in Congress by Madison, was opposed by Hamilton, who feared the loss of revenue from British imports. The movement in Congress for discrimination was strengthened by Jefferson's successive able reports on matters of commercial policy, but through the influence of Hamilton it was blocked in February 1791 and ultimately abandoned. Meanwhile, the secretary of the treasury had maintained a surprising intimacy with George Beckwith, the unofficial British representative (1789-1791), with whom the secretary of state properly refused to have anything to do.

Early in 1791, at the request of his chief, Jefferson drafted an opinion on the constitutionality of the measure creating the Bank of the United States. This had been passed by Congress at the insistence of Hamilton, but the power of the federal government to set up such a corporation had been denied by Attorney General Edmund Randolph and by Congressman James Madison. Jefferson agreed with them, holding that the powers assumed by Hamilton's bill were not among those enumerated as belonging to the federal government. Neither could they be properly derived from the general clauses, which he interpreted literally. While he believed that constitutions should be periodically revised, he insisted on their strict interpretation until formally modified. He granted little latitude to judges and was characteristically distrustful of strong government. In this instance, his fears were indirectly heightened by his growing distrust of Hamilton, who lusted for power and appeared to be interpreting the Constitution to suit himself. These objections were referred by Washington to Hamilton, who responded in a lengthy paper in which he ably championed the doctrine of liberal construction. After receiving this, the president signed the bill.

Despite his confidence in his own position, Jefferson had stated that, in deference to Congress, the president should not veto the bill unless thoroughly convinced of its unconstitutionality. Washington kept the opinions in his own hands, and they were not made public for many years. There is no reason to suppose he showed Hamilton's to

Jefferson, and the conflict over the construction of the Constitution was far from over. It was clear that the aggressive secretary of the treasury had won another victory.

In the spring of 1791, Thomas Paine's *Rights of Man* appeared in America, with an extract from a private note of Jefferson as a preface. His statement that he was glad that something was to be said publicly against "the political heresies" that had sprung up was interpreted both as an approval of Paine, who was anathema to the Anglophiles in America, and as a reflection on John Adams, whose expatiations on the faults of democratic systems Jefferson had indeed had in mind. Jefferson's statement of regret that he and his old friend had been "thrown on the public stage as public antagonists" may be accepted as sincere by others, as it was by Adams, but the incident identified Jefferson with criticism of the aristocratic tendencies of the government and in the end was politically advantageous to him. Fortuitous circumstances thus served to make a popular figure of one who abhorred controversy, who preferred to work behind the scenes, and who lacked the personal aggressiveness commonly associated with political leadership.

In May-June 1791 he and Madison made a botanical trip to New England, during which they doubtless gave some thought to politics; and, on 31 October, Philip Freneau published in Philadelphia the first number of the *National Gazette,* in opposition to the *Gazette of the United States,* published by John Fenno. Jefferson, knowing Freneau to be an ardent Republican, had given him the small post of translator in the Department of State. Hamilton had already given Fenno the more lucrative printing at his disposal and was later to give him personal financial assistance. With the increasingly bitter criticism of Hamilton in Congress during the winter of 1791-1792 Jefferson afterward claimed that he had nothing to do, except that he expressed hostility in conversation with, and letters to, his friends. Madison was the major organizer but Jefferson had become the symbol of anti-Hamiltonianism, and although more scrupulous of proprieties than his colleague, he served to inspire forces that he did not now or ever essay to command.

Hamilton had established with George Hammond, who presented in November 1791 his credentials as British minister, an intimacy similar to that which Beckwith had enjoyed. Hammond, forced by Jefferson to admit that he had no power to negotiate a new treaty, unwisely undertook to debate with the American secretary of state the infractions of the treaty of peace. Jefferson's magnificent reply of 29 May 1792, which completely demolished the mediocre case of the Britisher, was submitted in draft to

Hamilton and, with the latter's relatively minor criticism, to Washington, who heartily approved it. To Hammond, however, the secretary of the treasury lamented the "intemperate violence" of Jefferson and stated that the reply had not been read by Washington and did not represent the position of the government. Thus fortified by assurances that nullified Jefferson's arguments, the British minister submitted the matter to his superiors at home, who felt safe in ignoring it. The full extent of Hamilton's intrigue was not exposed until the twentieth century, but Jefferson was probably aware that he owed his undeserved defeat to his colleague.

By the summer of 1792 the hostility of the two men had become implacable. In the spring Jefferson had expressed in no uncertain terms to Washington his opinion that the causes of public discontent lay in Hamilton's policy, particularly in the "corruption" that had accompanied the financial measures of the latter and that had extended to the legislature itself. A formal list of the objections Jefferson had cited was submitted by the president to Hamilton on 29 July and was replied to by the latter three weeks later. In the meantime, Hamilton, smarting under the barbs of Freneau, had made an anonymous attack on the democratic editor and, through him, on Jefferson. Washington's letters to his two secretaries, deploring their dissensions within the government, elicited lengthy replies in which each man presented his case, not only to his chief but also to posterity. Washington did not succeed in stilling the troubled waters. During the autumn of 1792, Hamilton published in the newspapers a series of ferocious anonymous attacks on his colleague, with the definite object of driving him from office. Jefferson, with greater dignity or greater discretion, refrained from newspaper controversy, leaving his defense to his friends. He probably played a part, however, in drafting the resolutions of William Branch Giles, presented early in 1793, which were severely critical of Hamilton's conduct of the treasury.

Jefferson's hostility to Hamilton, apart from his justifiable resentment at the interference of the latter in the conduct of his department, was like that of a religious devotee to an enemy of his faith. In a letter to Washington of 9 September 1792, Jefferson said he was convinced that Hamilton's "system flowed from principles adverse to liberty, and was calculated to undermine and demolish the Republic, by creating an influence of his department over the members of the Legislature." Hamilton's hostility to Jefferson, apart from resentment that his own power had been challenged, was like that of a practical man of affairs who found specific projects impeded by one whom he regarded as a quibbling theorist. Washington valued both men and wanted both to remain in office, utilized both, and followed the policies of neither exclusively. The invaluable service rendered by each in his own field of activity vindicates the judgment of the patient president.

Yielding to the request of his chief, Jefferson remained in office until the last day of 1793, during a critical period of foreign affairs. Although the course of the revolution in France had been followed with growing concern by the conservative groups in America, popular opinion was still rather favorable to the French when the war in Europe was extended to Great Britain (1 February 1793) and a new French minister, Edmond Charles Genêt, came to the United States (8 April 1793). Jefferson was determined that his country should take no action that would imply opposition to the principles of the French Revolution or the repudiation of the French alliance, but he fully agreed with Washington and Hamilton that American neutrality was imperative. He successfully urged the avoidance of the word "neutrality" in Washington's proclamation, however, in order to offend the French as little as possible and in the hope of gaining commercial concessions from the British. He also prevailed upon Washington to receive Genêt without qualifications. Although Jefferson greeted Genêt kindly, rejoiced in the popular enthusiasm for democracy that the fiery emissary kindled, and, through a letter of introduction, came dangerously near conniving with the Frenchman in his projected expedition against Louisiana, he strove with diligence to maintain neutrality and bore with patience the immense labors that the American position imposed upon him. When Genêt persisted in offensive actions and criticisms, Jefferson lost patience with him. Agreeing with his colleagues that the man had become intolerable, he wrote a powerful letter asking Genêt's recall.

Although Jefferson protested vigorously against British infringements on American neutral rights during the war, he was unable as secretary of state to solve the problem of British relations. Jay's Treaty (1794), which was negotiated after his retirement under the influence of Hamilton, was regarded by Jefferson as an ignominious surrender of American claims. The negotiations instituted by him with Spain were equally unsuccessful during his term of office, but the American objectives that he had formulated were attained in Pinckney's Treaty (Treaty of San Lorenzo) of 1795. If in the heat of the

Jefferson's sketch of Monticello before the remodeling of 1796. (Thomas Jefferson Foundation.)

controversy with Hamilton he was at times guilty of extravagant assertion, he performed an inestimable service to the republic by calling attention to the dangers of his colleague's policy, by formulating the chief grounds of opposition to it, and by inspiring the forces that were to effect its modification after it had achieved its most significant results.

Now in his fifty-first year, Jefferson believed that his second retirement from public life was final. Soon he resumed building operations at Monticello, following revised plans that had grown out of his architectural observations abroad. By a system of crop rotation he tried to restore his wasted lands. He experimented with mechanical devices, built a gristmill, set up a nail factory, and directed his large but relatively unprofitable establishment with characteristic diligence and attention to minute details. His renewed and increased enthusiasm for agriculture quite got the better of his love of study. At no other period of his mature life, perhaps, did he read so little and write so rarely. His days on horseback soon restored his health to the vigor that he feared it had permanently lost, and he brought some order into his tangled finances. During his years as a national officeholder he had largely lived on his small salary, yet the profits from his plantations and even sales of slaves and lands had been insufficient to rid him of the old

Wayles debt, which in 1795 was increased by a judgment against the executors as security for the late Richard Randolph. Like so many of his fellow Virginians, Jefferson was unable to realize on his assets and was eaten up by interest to British creditors. Nonetheless, his personal generosity was unabated.

To Madison, whom he regarded as the logical Republican candidate for the presidency, he wrote on 27 April 1795 that the "little spice of ambition" he had had in his younger days had long since evaporated and that the question of his own candidacy was forever closed. He remained, however, the symbol and the prophet of a political faith. When the leaders of his party determined to support him in 1796, he did not gainsay them, but he was surprisingly content to run second to Adams, who was his senior and whom he perhaps regarded as the only barrier against Hamilton.

The vice-presidency provided a salary that Jefferson undoubtedly needed, enabled him to spend much time at Monticello, and afforded him relative leisure. The chief significance of his service as presiding officer of the Senate lies in the fact that out of it emerged his *Manual of Parliamentary Practice* (1801), subsequently published in many editions and translated into several languages and still the basis of parliamentary usage in the Senate. Despite the conciliatory spirit that marked his early relations with Adams, Jefferson played no part in the conduct of the administration, in which the hand of Hamilton was soon apparent.

As vice-president, Jefferson was characteristically discreet in public utterance, but his general attitude toward the questions of the day was undoubtedly well known; and he was inevitably the target of the Federalist press, which continued to regard him as the personification of his party. The publication in the United States in May 1797 of a private letter of his to Philip Mazzei (24 April 1796), which originally appeared in a Florentine paper and was somewhat altered in form by successive translations, gave wide currency to his earlier criticisms of the Federalists. It was interpreted by many as an attack on Washington. Jefferson made no effort to disavow a letter that was in substance his, suffering in silence while the Federalist press termed him "libeler," "liar," and "assassin."

He had approved of the conduct of James Monroe as minister to France, which aroused much hostile Federalist comment, and believed that the bellicose spirit which swept the country after the publication of the "XYZ dispatches" was aggravated by the

Hamiltonians, with a view to advancing their own interests and embroiling the United States on the side of the British. He himself was sympathetic with Elbridge Gerry, the commissioner who proved more amenable than his colleagues to French influence, and suggested that Gerry publish an account of his experiences, but Jefferson had no enthusiasm for the existing order in France. He was glad to drop the disastrous French issue when, at the height of the war fever, the Federalists provided a better one by passing the Alien and Sedition Acts. Jefferson rightly regarded hysterical hostility to aliens, such as his friends C. F. Volney and Joseph Priestley, and attacks upon freedom of speech as menacing the ideals he most cherished. Since the Sedition Act was applied chiefly to Republican editors, partisan as well as philosophical motives were conjoined in his opposition to it.

His most notable contribution to the campaign of discussion consisted of the Kentucky Resolutions of 1798. (His authorship was not disclosed until years later.) The Virginia Resolutions, drawn by Madison, were similar in tenor though more moderate. The constitutional doctrines advanced by Jefferson—that the government of the United States originated in a compact, that acts of the federal government unauthorized by the delegated powers are void, and that a state has the right to judge of infractions of its powers and to determine the mode of redress—were much emphasized in later years. His dominant purpose, however, was to attack the offensive laws as an unconstitutional and unwarranted infringement upon individual freedom, a denial of rights that could not be alienated. The language of what was in effect a party platform was in the nature of the case extravagant, but Jefferson and Madison had no intention of carrying matters to extremes. More important from the practical point of view than any promulgation of constitutional theory was the vindication of the right of public discussion and political opposition.

Nominated by a congressional caucus for the presidency and by no means indifferent to the outcome as he had been four years earlier, Jefferson owed his success in the election of 1800 as much to Federalist dissensions as to any formal issues that had been raised. To the Republican victory, his running mate, Aaron Burr, made no small contribution. By fault of the electoral machinery, soon to be remedied, the two Republicans received an identical vote and the choice of a president was left to the House of Representatives. Despite the personal hostility to Jefferson of the High Federalists, who voted for Burr to the end, the opinion (to which Hamilton contributed) that Jefferson was the safer man of the two caused the House ultimately to yield to the unquestionable desire of the Republicans and to elect him.

Jefferson's diffidence and lack of spectacular qualities would have constituted in a later day a grave political handicap. His popular success was due in considerable part to his identification of himself with causes for which time was fighting—notably the broadening of the political base—and to his remarkable sensitivity to fluctuations in public opinion. As a practical politician, he worked through other men, whom he energized and who gave him to an extraordinary degree their devoted cooperation. His leadership was due not to self-assertiveness and imperiousness of will but to the fact that circumstances had made him a symbolic figure and that to an acute intelligence and unceasing industry he joined a dauntless and contagious faith. The long struggle between his partisans and the Federalists has been variously interpreted as one between democracy and aristocracy, state rights and nationalism, agrarianism and capitalism. In retrospective old age, he referred to the "revolution" of 1800, comparing it to that of 1776. He may have exaggerated the importance of the victory of his party. At the least, however, it signified vindication of political opposition, the repudiation of a reactionary faction, and the accession of more representative leaders to power.

Jefferson, the first president to be inaugurated in Washington, had himself drawn a plan for the city, part of which survives in the Mall. As secretary of state, to whom the commissioners of the District of Columbia were responsible, he had suggested the competition for the new federal buildings and he was considerably responsible for the selection of classical designs. As president, he appointed Benjamin H. Latrobe surveyor of public buildings and fully cooperated in planning for the future development of a monumental city. In his day, pomp and ceremony, to which on principle and for political reasons he was opposed, would have been preposterous in the wilderness village. Remaining until the last at Conrad's boardinghouse, where his democratic simplicity was marked, he walked to the nearby Senate chamber of the uncompleted Capitol, to receive the oath of office from his distant cousin and inveterate political foe Chief Justice John Marshall. Although aware of the last efforts of the Federalists to entrench themselves in the judiciary, he believed that after the long "contest of opinion" the danger of monarchy was now removed, and in his benevolent inaugural he sought to make acquiescence in the will of the majority as easy as possible. Although he challenged the asser-tion that a republican government could not be strong, he defined its functions as sharply limited. It should restrain men from injuring one another, he said, but otherwise leave them to regulate their own concerns. He declared against special privileges and urged encouragement, not of industry, but of agriculture and of commerce "as its handmaid." He reiterated his conviction that the federal government should chiefly concern itself with foreign affairs, leaving to the states the administration of local matters.

Inaugurated in his fifty-eighth year, he made his official residence in the boxlike and incompletely plastered President's House, though he continued to spend as much time as possible at Monticello, where he was still directing building operations. His beautiful second daughter, Maria, now the wife of her cousin John Wayles Eppes, had also by this time made him a grandfather. (She was to sadden her father's life by her untimely death in 1804.) Generally deprived of adequate feminine supervision while in Washington, Jefferson lived there in sartorial indifference and dispensed generous but informal hospitality, as he was accustomed to do at home, to the consternation of dip-lomats jealous of precedence. After he had overcome his initial diffidence, his manners were easy. To hostile observers his democratic simplicity was a pose. To his friends it was the naturalness of one who had achieved and thought enough to dare to be himself. His loose gait and habit of lounging, together with his discursive though highly infor-mative conversation, doubtless contributed to the common but erroneous impression among his foes that this most scholarly of statesmen was a careless thinker. "His external appearance," according to his ardent admirer Margaret Bayard Smith, "had no pretentions to elegance, but it was neither coarse nor awkward, and it must be owned his greatest personal attraction was a countenance beaming with benevolence and intelligence."

Chief in his harmonious official family were James Madison, the secretary of state, and Albert Gallatin, who as secretary of the treasury was to carry out with consid-erable success his program of economy. Jefferson found the federal establishment com-pletely dominated by Federalists and clearly recognized the desirability of attaining a balance. This could be done only by removals, for, as he said, vacancies "by death are few; by resignation none." Judicial officers were removable only by established process, but other civil officials were appointed at the pleasure of the president and were thus removable by him. Early in his administration Jefferson stated publicly that he would have to avail himself of this unquestionable authority and would appoint only Republicans to office. He had not fully restored the balance by the middle of his first term, but he then felt warranted in leaving the creation of vacancies to the course of nature. Although no nonpartisan policy was adopted and the Republicans eventually came to dominate the establishment as the Federalists had done, the standards of the federal service were fully maintained.

Jefferson abandoned the custom of delivering messages to Congress in person, and he carefully avoided the appearance of dictating to that body. Until almost the end of his administration, however, he maintained over Congress indirect and tactful but efficacious control. The Republicans were the majority in both houses, and despite occasional minor revolts, he fully maintained his leadership of the party. During most of his presidency, the floor leader of the House was recognized as his spokesman.

The repeal of the excise taxes early in 1802 redounded to the popularity of the administration. At this time the Western world was enjoying a temporary period of peace, and a reduction in military and naval appropriations seemed to be warranted. In 1802 the repeal of the Judiciary Act of 1801 followed Jefferson's recommendation. That act, which had been described as the last word of the Federalist system, was not without merit, but it was clearly designed to perpetuate Federalist dominance of the federal judiciary. In the case of *Marbury* v. *Madison* (1803), Chief Justice Marshall rebuked the president for withholding the commission of the justices of the peace appointed by John Adams in the last hours of his presidency. This rebuke attracted far more attention at the time than the declaration that a minor provision of an act of Congress was unconstitutional. In Republican opinion the motivation of the chief justice was suspect, and the transcendent authority of the judiciary over the legislative and executive branches of the government was not conceded. Jefferson undoubtedly regarded himself as authorized to judge of the propriety of his own conduct. His responsibility was to the people, not the Court.

In pardoning victims of the Sedition Act, Jefferson pronounced that statute unconstitutional, as he believed he was called upon to do. He approved of the use of the weapon of impeachment against Samuel Chase, a notoriously partisan justice, and deeply regretted its failure. Though the federal judges learned to observe the proprieties better, they did not cease to be political. Jefferson never receded from his position that the

Federalists, from the battery of the immovable judiciary, were endeavoring to beat down the works of Republicanism and defeat the will of the people.

By the spring of 1802, Jefferson became alarmed by reports of the retrocession of the province of Louisiana to France by Spain. In a private letter of 18 April 1802 to Robert R. Livingston, the American minister in Paris, he said that the possessor of New Orleans was the natural enemy of the United States and that by placing itself there France would assume an attitude of defiance. He was now willing to ally himself with his old British foes if the mouth of the Mississippi should fall under the control of the nation that Napoleon had made the most aggressive in the world. The Spanish, who were weaker and more compliant, had granted to Americans, in Pinckney's Treaty of 1795, the right of deposit in New Orleans. The revocation of this by the Spanish intendant on 16 October 1802 created a crisis in the West. In fact, this was an independent action and was afterward reversed, but it was commonly blamed on the French. There was warlike talk in Congress, and Jefferson was not averse to the ultimate resort to force if necessary to keep the Mississippi open. But he still hoped to meet this crisis by diplomacy.

Early in 1803 he appointed James Monroe special envoy to France and secured from Congress an appropriation of $2 million. By secret agreement this fund might be used to purchase the "island" of New Orleans. The hopes of the administration extended to West Florida and, in lesser degree, to East Florida. The treaty that Monroe and Livingston signed on 30 April 1803 provided for the purchase of the entire province of Louisiana for approximately $15 million. They had achieved a diplomatic triumph of the first magnitude and made an extraordinary bargain, but the sheer size of the cession and certain provisions of the treaty created perplexities and problems.

Before dispatching Monroe, Jefferson, as a strict constructionist, had raised the question of the constitutional authority of the federal government to acquire territory. His colleagues, especially Gallatin, had assured him that because the United States was a sovereign nation, the federal government had that power. He dismissed his doubts at the time, but they were revived when he learned that his representative had not merely acquired the island of New Orleans but had doubled the area of the country. The treaty specifically required the incorporation of a vast region and the granting to its inhabitants all the rights and privileges of American citizens. This would ultimately effect a change

The Entrance Hall at Monticello, crowded with natural history specimens, maps, works of art, and a variety of artifacts, served as a reception hall and museum to educate Jefferson's visitors. (Photograph by Robert C. Lautman.)

in the Union which the fathers of the Constitution had not anticipated or provided for. Jefferson believed that a fresh grant of power in the form of a constitutional amendment was called for and made at least two attempts to draft one. None of his counselors and supporters appears to have seen any need for an amendment, however, and, while it was generally agreed that an amendment would have been readily adopted, there was not enough time to go through the prescribed procedure. To be effective, the treaty had to be ratified within six months. Furthermore, the report reached Jefferson that Napoleon now regretted having ratified the treaty and would tolerate no change in it. Jefferson's constitutional scruples were voiced in private to his own supporters. The treaty was approved and put into effect against the opposition of Federalist die-hards but with overwhelming public approval.

The Louisiana Purchase provides a striking example of Jefferson's pragmatic statesmanship. By means of it, he assured the physical greatness of his country and the future success of his party, as exemplified by his own triumphant reelection. Western discontent was largely stilled, and the Federalists were reduced to sectional impotence. For all of this, his momentary theoretical inconsistency seemed to his partisans a small price to pay and later historians have exaggerated its significance. The purchase served to facilitate the expedition for which he had already commissioned Meriwether Lewis. For this, he himself prepared elaborate instructions. No one rejoiced more than he in the discoveries made by Lewis and William Clark. He afterward wrote the best biographical account of Lewis, his former secretary.

Livingston and Monroe had bought a vaguely defined region that they soon persuaded themselves included West Florida. Jefferson subsequently embodied similar views in a pamphlet that determined the attitude of the administration and its supporters. The Louisiana revenue act that came to be known as the Mobile Act of 24 February 1804 assumed the acquisition of West Florida, but Jefferson, finding that the Spanish were not acquiescent as he had expected, practically annulled its offensive features by proclamation and sent Monroe on what proved to be a futile mission to Spain. The perplexing question of West Florida remained unsettled during Jefferson's administration, and his tortuous efforts to acquire this coveted region served only to weaken his position in Congress and his hand abroad.

His policy of peaceable negotiation did not extend to the Barbary pirates, to whom he applied more force than had any previous American president. Following the repudiation of a treaty by the bey of Tripoli in 1801, Jefferson dispatched against him a naval force, which blockaded his ports. Subsequently Jefferson employed naval force against the sultan of Morocco. The treaty at length negotiated with Tripoli granted the United States the most favorable terms yet given any nation by that piratical power.

Jefferson was slow in becoming alarmed by the mystifying movement of his former vice-president, Aaron Burr, in the West, but on 27 November 1806, he issued a proclamation of warning against an illegal expedition against the dominions of Spain. He was now convinced of the existence of a conspiracy and was aware that its objectives might extend to the separation of the trans-Allegheny region from the Union. In January, responding to a congressional resolution, he described the actions he had taken and communicated a copy of an incriminating letter from Burr to Gen. James Wilkinson that he had just received from the latter. Presumably with a view to justifying his own actions, Jefferson stated that Burr's guilt was unquestionable. Thus, he left himself open to the charge of prejudging the case. Furthermore, many people were highly distrustful of Wilkinson, who had been ordered to New Orleans to stop Burr's expedition if it got that far and had been guilty of high-handed and arbitrary actions there against individuals whom he suspected. News of these actions was received in Washington before the failure of Burr's enterprise was reported there. By order of Gov. Edward Tiffin of Ohio, boats and supplies that Burr had caused to be assembled were captured at Blennerhassett's Island in the Ohio River. Burr himself joined the remnant of the expedition at the mouth of the Cumberland, and it came to an inglorious end in Mississippi. Opponents of the administration, taking up the cause of Burr, claimed that the danger had been greatly exaggerated and that the prosecution of Burr was actually persecution at the hands of a vindictive president.

The trial of Burr for treason in Richmond before Chief Justice Marshall in the summer of 1807 was one of the most extraordinary in American history. Among its more notable features were the issuance of two subpoenas ordering the president to produce documents, the unmeasured denunciation of the president by Burr's counsel, especially by the "Federal Bulldog," Luther Martin, and the near escape of General Wilkinson from indictment. The grand jury indicted Burr for both treason and misdemeanor for causing the assemblage at Blennerhassett's Island. The chief justice, reversing the position he had recently taken in another case regarding treasonable conduct, now ruled that the physical presence of the accused at the scene of the crime was required. Burr had not been at Blennerhassett's Island, and Marshall did not allow the prosecution to present the evidence of his actions elsewhere. Burr's acquittal on both counts was thus made inevitable. Not without warrant did a prominent Republican say that the chief justice acquitted Burr. Marshall was critical of Jefferson throughout the extremely political proceedings. Jefferson believed that there had been a miscarriage of justice but had no thoughts of resorting to impeachment. He observed the proprieties better than Marshall did. He would not have done his duty if he had not caused Burr to be prosecuted. He always believed that Wilkinson had done the country a service in revealing the conspiracy, but he went too far in his support of that tattered warrior.

The difficulties that Jefferson faced during his second term as the head of a neutral nation in a time of ruthless European war could probably have been successfully met by no American statesman. Until 1805 the British had in practice granted sufficient concessions from their commercial regulations to permit prosperity to the American carrying trade, but following the *Essex* decision of that year, they tightened their control of commerce and seized many American vessels. Also, the impressment of seamen remained a grievance, which the British would do nothing to remove. Then, in the battle between British orders in council and Napoleonic decrees, the neutral American Republic, unable to meet both sets of requirements and threatened with the confiscation of commercial vessels in case of violation, was placed in an intolerable position.

Of the possible courses of action open to him, war did not commend itself to Jefferson, who did not want to take sides with either of the European rivals. After the *Leopard* fired on the *Chesapeake* in June 1807, a declaration of war against the British might have been supported by the American people. Jefferson issued a proclamation that denied to British armed vessels the hospitality of American waters. He gave the British government the opportunity to disavow the outrage, but they responded to this by prolonged procrastination. He had previously sent William Pinkney to London to serve with Monroe on a mission extraordinary, and had tried to strengthen the hands of the negotiators by the Non-Importation Act of 1806, which was to become effective some months later. His reliance was on diplomacy, supplemented by the threat of economic pressure, and when diplomacy failed (as it did in the unacceptable Monroe-Pinkney treaty), he fell back on economic pressure.

Because of the intensification of the conflict between the two great powers and the increased infringement on American rights by both of them in the summer and autumn of 1807, some sort of governmental action seemed unavoidable. Jefferson recommended the embargo as the least evil of his options. Its immediate purpose was defensive—to keep American ships and seamen out of this conflict. It came to be regarded increasingly as an offensive weapon by means of which concessions could be gained. Adopted in December 1807, after an inadequate debate and by an overwhelming vote because of the dominance of Congress by Jefferson's party, the measure combined with the Non-Intercourse Act to bring about a theoretical suspension of foreign commerce without a specified limit of time.

The attempts to enforce the embargo involved an exercise of unexampled economic authority by the federal government and an inevitable and increasing infringement on individual rights, which were contrary to Jefferson's most cherished ideals. He and Gallatin, the chief enforcement officer, exercised no authority beyond what was granted by successive acts of Congress, and while regretting the hardships attributable to the provisions of embargo, Jefferson had expected them to be endured as they would have been in wartime. He had not anticipated the degree of resistance in commercial districts or the rank crop of corruption that sprang up. His political enemies undoubtedly made things harder for him and Gallatin, but he blamed them unduly for the failure of enforcement. He claimed, with considerable justification, that the embargo was not in effect long enough to attain its objectives, and it may well be that under other circumstances some measure of the sort might have proved an efficacious weapon. But in 1808-1809, employed by a weak power, it served chiefly to impoverish the sections that supported Jefferson most loyally, to give a new lease on life to partisan opposition in New England, and to bring a memorable administration to an inglorious close. Forced to yield to a rebellious Congress, on 1 March 1809 he signed the Non-Intercourse Act, which replaced the embargo. Shortly afterward he turned the presidential office over to his friend and colleague James Madison with unquestionable relief. He described himself as a waveworn mariner approaching the shore, as a prisoner emerging from shackles, and declared that Nature had intended him for the tranquil pursuits of science, in which he found supreme delight.

During the past eight years this earnest advocate of the freedom of the press had been subjected to a flood of personal calumny. Long regarded in ecclesiastical circles, especially in New England, as the embodiment of French infidelity, he not unnaturally aroused a storm of indignation, soon after his first inauguration, by offering to Thomas Paine passage to America on a sloop of war and by expressing the hope that his "useful labours" would be continued. The following year an indefensible assault was launched by a disgruntled pamphleteer to whom Jefferson had previously made monetary gifts that he himself designated as charity but that could be readily interpreted as a form of subsidy. To the charges of personal immorality made in 1802 by James Thomson Callender in the Richmond *Recorder*, almost every discreditable story reflecting on Jefferson's private life can be traced. Given nationwide currency by the Federalist press, these were discussed in 1805 in the legislative assembly of Massachusetts, where a motion to dismiss the printers of the assembly for publishing in the *New-England Palladium* (18 January 1805) libels on the president failed of adoption. One only of these charges was admitted by Jefferson. This referred to improper proposals of his to the wife of his friend John Walker, while he was yet a young man and single. For these he made restitution. The sensational story of his illicit relations with his slave Sally Hemings is without historical foundation and is wholly out of character. As Henry Adams said, Jefferson, a model husband and father, was "more refined than many women in the delicacy of his private relations."

For the wide acceptance, by persons of the better sort, of the extravagant charges of an unscrupulous drunkard, the sensitive president was disposed to blame his old theological foes, especially in New England. There his followers were assaulting the ancient alliance between church and state, for the final overthrow of which they deserve considerable credit. It may well be, as Henry Adams said, that Jefferson did not understand the New Englanders, but it is certain that they did not understand him. Though sanguine in temperament, he was as serious-minded and almost as devoid of humor as any Puritan, and had he lived a generation later, he would have been more at home in liberal religious circles in New England than anywhere else in America. At many times he paid grateful tribute to Epicurus and Epictetus, but as early as 1803 he began to select from the Gospels the passages that he believed to have come from Jesus. Toward the end of his life this amateur higher critic placed parallel texts, in four languages, in a "wee-little book," which he entitled *The Life and Morals of Jesus of Nazareth*. This was not published until the twentieth century. He regarded himself as a "real Christian," since he followed what he believed to be the teachings of Jesus.

During the last seventeen years of his life, Jefferson did not leave Virginia. The embargo and its aftermath were ruinous to him, as to many Virginia planters, and because of the demands of incessant hospitality, he could not live as simply as he desired. After the War of 1812, however, the sale of his library of some sixty-five hundred volumes to the government, for the Library of Congress, served to relieve his financial burdens somewhat; and his grandson, Thomas Jefferson Randolph, took over the management of his lands. Laborious correspondence occupied a disproportionate amount of his time, but he enjoyed exchanging ideas with John Adams (with whom his old friendship was beautifully restored), with Lafayette, Pierre-Samuel Du Pont de Nemours, and many others. In the letters of these years he has left a mine of treasure. He gave his counsel to Madison and Monroe when they asked it; and some of his expressions on public policy, as on the Missouri Compromise and on the attitude of the United States toward Europe and the Latin American republics, are notable.

The chief public problem to which he addressed himself was that of education in Virginia, which he continued to call his "country." He never ceased to advocate a comprehensive statewide system of public education, such as he had proposed in 1779. "Enlighten the people generally," he wrote Du Pont de Nemours on 24 April 1816, "and tyranny and oppressions of both mind and body will vanish like evil spirits at the dawn of day." Popular education he regarded as more than a defensive weapon and a guarantor of freedom. His proposals of 1779 had been marked by a unique provision whereby youths of great promise were to be advanced from one grade of instruction to another without cost, and he hoped that these "geniuses … raked from the rubbish" would serve as statesmen or would enlarge the domains of human knowledge. He formulated, as perhaps no other American of his generation, an educational philosophy for a democratic state; and in his last years he declared himself in favor of a literacy test for citizenship.

Having failed in his earlier efforts to transform the College of William and Mary, by 1800 Jefferson had hopes of establishing in the more salubrious upper country a university on a broad, liberal, and modern plan. Whatever interest he may have had, during his presidency, in the creation of a national university contingent upon the amendment of the Constitution, Virginia was central to all his thoughts after 1809. Indeed, his regret that so many of his "countrymen" went to be educated among "foreigners" (as at Princeton) or were taught at home by "beggars" (northern tutors) was partly due to the fear that their political principles were being contaminated. His representations may have stimulated Gov. John Tyler to send to the Assembly in 1809 his strong message on education, which resulted in the establishment, the following year, of the Literary Fund. Jefferson regarded this as an inadequate provision for general education, but it later made possible the creation of an institution of higher learning.

By happy chance, Jefferson in 1814 became associated as a trustee with the unorganized Albemarle Academy. Transformed into Central College, this became the germ from which the University of Virginia developed, under his adroit management at every stage. His letter of 7 September 1814 to Peter Carr, outlining in masterly fashion his views of a state system, may have inspired the resolution adopted by the General Assembly on 24 February 1816, which required a report on a scheme of public instruction.

Shortly thereafter, Jefferson himself drafted a bill that contained most of the features of his more famous proposal of 1779 and included a provision for a university. This was rejected, and for a time it appeared that after an appropriation for elementary schools no funds would be available for a higher institution. At length, in 1818, by a compromise, appropriations were authorized for elementary schools (though not for intermediate schools) and for a university.

Jefferson was appointed a member, and became chairman, of the Rockfish Gap Commission, empowered to recommend a site. By skillful use of geographical arguments, he gained the victory for Central College in August 1818. The report, which he had drafted beforehand, incorporated his ideas of what a university should be and remains one of his greatest educational papers. After a legislative battle in which he acted only behind the scenes, the report was adopted, and in 1819 the University of Virginia was chartered. It opened its doors in 1825. Though the services of Joseph C. Cabell and John H. Cocke in launching the institution were invaluable, Jefferson, who was inevitably appointed a member of the first board of visitors and elected rector, remained until his death the dominant factor in its affairs. He received architectural suggestions from Benjamin H. Latrobe and, to a lesser extent, William Thornton, but the plan of an "academical village" was his own. Many of the specifications were drawn up by him and the "pavilions," "hotels," dormitories, colonnades, and arcades were constructed under his supervision. At his death, only the Rotunda, modeled by him on the Pantheon at Rome, was incomplete.

Upon the organization of the institution, he left his most characteristic impression perhaps in the establishment of independent, diploma-conferring "schools," in the provision for entire freedom in the election of courses, in the complete disregard of the conventional grouping of students in classes, and in the provision for a rotating chairmanship of the faculty, without a president. Despite his insistence that Republican, rather than Federalist, principles be taught, to a remarkable extent he freed the institution from hampering restriction and made it in spirit a university. Though he was disappointed in his full hopes of drawing from the Old World to the faculty "the first characters in science," the mission of his young friend Francis Walker Gilmer to Great Britain to procure professors was measurably successful. The new institution had from the outset a flavor of cosmopolitanism, and several of the first professors achieved distinction. The "Old Sachem" lived to see the university opened in 1825 and for more than a year in operation.

During his lifetime, Jefferson received not only American but also international recognition as a man, and as a patron, of learning. Elected president of the American Philosophical Society on 6 January 1797, he remained the head of this notable organization until 1815 and actively cooperated with it in the advancement and dissemination of knowledge. By introducing to his colleagues, on 10 March 1797, his megalonyx he fired the "signal gun of American paleontology." To them he read on 4 May 1798 a description of a moldboard of least resistance for a plow, for which invention he received in 1805 a gold medal from a French agricultural society. In due course he became associated with an extraordinary number of important societies in various countries of Europe, as he had long been with the chief learned, and almost all the agricultural, societies of America. On 26 December 1801 he was elected a foreign associate of the Institute of France. This signal honor, which during his lifetime was shared by no other man of American birth and residence, may best be attributed to his reputation in France as the most conspicuous American intellectual. He himself interpreted it as "an evidence of the brotherly spirit of Science, which unites into one family all its votaries of whatever grade, and however widely dispersed throughout the different quarters of the globe." He corresponded throughout his life with an extraordinary number of scientists and philosophers in other lands, as well as in America, and sought to make available in his own country the best of foreign thought and discovery.

Modern scholars have recognized Jefferson as an American pioneer in numerous branches of science, notably paleontology, ethnology, geography, and botany. Living before the age of specialization, he was for his day a careful investigator, no more credulous than his learned contemporaries, and notable among them for his effort in all fields to attain scientific exactitude. In state papers he is commonly the lawyer, pleading a cause; in the heat of political controversy he may have compromised his intellectual ideals and certainly indulged in exaggeration at times; but his procedure in arriving at his fundamental opinions, the habits of his life, and his temperament were essentially those of a scholar. As secretary of state, he was in effect the first commissioner of patents and the first patent examiner. He himself invented or adapted to personal uses numerous ingenious devices.

At home in French, Italian, and Spanish, as well as Greek and Latin, he wrote *An Essay Towards Facilitating Instruction in the Anglo-Saxon and Modern Dialects of the English Language* (published in 1851); and during a generation he amassed a large collection of Indian vocabularies, only to have them cast upon the waters by thieves in 1809. He owned one of the best private collections of paintings and statuary in the country, and he has been termed by Fiske Kimball "the first American connoisseur and patron of the arts." Besides the Virginia state capitol, Monticello, and the original buildings of the University of Virginia, he designed wholly or in part numerous Virginia houses, among them his own Poplar Forest, Farmington, and Barboursville. Before the advent of professional architects in America, he began to collect books on architecture and discovered Palladio, from whom his careful and extensive observations abroad never weaned him. He did more than any other man to stimulate the classical revival in America. His own work, while always ingenious, is academic, precise, and orderly, but because of the fortunate necessity of using brick and wood, the new creation was a blend, with a pleasing domesticity. He created a definite school of builders in Virginia; sought to establish formal instruction in architecture; stimulated and encouraged, among others, Charles Bulfinch and William Thornton; and, except for the fact that he accepted no pay for his services, was as truly professional as they. It is probably no exaggeration to say with Kimball that he was "the father of our national architecture."

Few other American statesmen have been such careful and unremitting students of political thought and history as Jefferson was, or more concerned with ultimate ends. Yet he has left no treatise on political philosophy, and all general statements about his theoretical position are subject to qualification. He was always more interested in applications than in speculation, and he was forced to modify his own philosophy in practice. But, despite unquestionable inconsistencies, his major aims and the general trend of his policies are unmistakable. A homely aristocrat in manner of life and personal tastes, he distrusted all rulers and feared the rise of an industrial proletariat, but more than any of his eminent contemporaries, he trusted the common man, if measurably enlightened and kept in rural virtue. Though pained and angered when the free press made him the victim of its license, he was a passionate advocate of human liberty and laid supreme stress on the individual. Though he clearly realized the value of union, he emphasized the importance of the states and of local agencies of government. An intellectual internationalist, he gave wholehearted support to the policy of political isolation and anticipated the development on the North American continent of a dominant nation, unique in civilization. A philosophical statesman rather than a political philosopher, he contributed to democracy and liberalism a faith rather than a body of doctrine. By his works alone he must be adjudged one of the greatest of all Americans, while the influence of his energizing faith is immeasurable.

By the very contradictions of his subtle and complex personality, of his bold mind and highly sensitive nature, Jefferson has both vexed and fascinated all who have attempted to interpret him. As Henry Adams said in his *History of the United States*, "Almost every other American statesman might be described in a parenthesis. A few broad strokes of the brush would paint the portraits of all the early Presidents with this exception … ; but Jefferson could be painted only touch by touch, with a fine pencil, and the perfection of the likeness depended upon the shifting and uncertain flicker of its semi-transparent shadows."

The last years of this most enigmatical and probably most versatile of great Americans were marked by philosophical serenity in the face of impending financial disaster. Ruined by the failure in 1819 of his friend Wilson Cary Nicholas, whose notes for $20,000 he had endorsed, he tried vainly to find a purchaser for his lands and secured legislative permission, in the last year of his life, to dispose of most of them by the common method of a lottery. The public strongly protested against this indignity to him and some voluntary contributions were made, so the project was ultimately abandoned. Jefferson died believing that his debts would be paid, fortunately not realizing that Monticello was soon to pass from the hands of his heirs forever. A beloved and revered patriarch in the extensive family circle, he retained extraordinary intellectual vigor and rode his horse daily until almost the end of his ordered and temperate life. His death occurred, with dramatic appropriateness, on the fiftieth anniversary of the Declaration of Independence, shortly after noon and a few hours before that of John Adams. His daughter Martha Randolph, with ten of her children and their progeny, and his grandson Francis Eppes survived him. On the simple stone over his grave in the family burial ground at Monticello, he is described as he wished to be remembered, not as the holder of great offices, but as the author of the Declaration of Independence and the Virginia statute for religious freedom, and as the father of the University of Virginia.

INDEX